The Power of the PEAKS

The 07.55 Newcastle to Liverpool express coasts round the sharp curve with canted track at Church Fenton, whilst a track maintenance gang stand back to let the train pass.

E. Sanderson

The Power of the PEAKS

Compiled by

Keith Montague

Oxford Publishing Co · Oxford

© Oxford Publishing Co. 1978

SBN 902888 99 4

Printed by Blackwell's
in the City of Oxford

No. 44 002 *Helvellyn* clears Westhouses with an evening freight on 9th August 1977.

L.P. Gater

Published by
Oxford Publishing Co.,
8 The Roundway,
Headington, Oxford.

INTRODUCTION

This book is the third in the series and a companion volume to the already published volumes on British Diesel locomotives, namely *The Power of the Deltics* and *The Power of the Westerns*, and in it shows the wider area where the 'Peaks' are and were used.

In this volume I have tried to cover the class 44, 45 and 46's from their early days to the present time, in a variety of locations on different types of trains spread over the British Rail network far and wide.

The 'Peak' story began in the late 1950's when British Rail made the decision to construct at Derby and Crewe a new type of locomotive for heavy main line passenger, and to a lesser extent, freight work. In 1959 the first class 44 locomotive No. D1 *Scafell Pike* entered traffic to be followed in quick succession by others of the same type and the slightly modified designs of the class 45 and 46's. The locomotives soon became known as 'Peaks' following the naming of all the class 44's after famous peaks. These locomotives are, in fact, among the heaviest types on British Rail with weights between 133 and 138 tons. Their official maximum speed is 90 mph, but the tractive effort is a massive 70,000 lb which is considerably more than even a Type 55 'Deltic'. At the design stage it was felt that such a weight required an eight-wheel bogie to spread the load and as with the slightly earlier class 40's a 1 Co-Co 1 wheel arrangement was devised. The outside axle on each bogie was thus an 'idle' carrier only.

The class 44's were built with nose end communicating doors and not provided with headcode indicator panels, display discs being used instead. On the later model class 45 and 46's the communicating door facilities were not provided but indicator panels were. The first headcode indicators consisted of two separate boxes, one each side of the front of the locomotive and the characters had to be altered by the handles underneath, which necessitated a somewhat precarious stance perched on the buffer beam. On the later models the integral centre indicators were included, which could be changed much more easily from inside the driver's cab. With the recent obsolescence of route displays on locomotives generally, the appearance has been further altered by the filling in of the panels and the substitution of two marker lights.

When delivered the first examples were in Brunswick green with a distinctive white band running the length of the locomotive at footplate level. In the early 1960's a yellow warning panel was painted on the nose end and this was later extended to cover the whole nose and bonnet of the engines. With the introduction of the British Rail Corporate Identity from 1965 all locomotives acquired a standard blue livery, and the now familiar double arrow symbol.

The class 44's have for some years been confined to freight-only duties and now have no steam heating boilers. All are based on Toton Motive Power depot, and their main work consists of hauling heavy coal traffic over Midland routes. The 45 and 46's provide power for passenger and freight trains and although some are now approaching 20 years of age, they remain untouched by withdrawals at the time of writing. A number of class 44's have, sadly, been taken out of service.

The first 'Peaks' invaded the Midland line ousting the then familiar Jubilees, Black 5's and Britannias which had dealt with the vast majority of passenger workings between St Pancras and the North. Although not immune from teething troubles, the reliability of the 'Peaks' made the sighting of steam substitutes somewhat rare. By the mid 1960's steam had been eliminated from this route and the diesels permitted a vastly improved and accelerated timetable. As more locomotives of this type became available for traffic, their field of operation spread quite considerably and today they can be seen in many parts of the country on both freight and passenger duties. Despite the gradual influx of class 47's during the 1960's the 'Peaks' are still entrusted with the majority of passenger and freight trains on the Midland route and for some years have been the mainstay of the North East — South West cross country services from places like Edinburgh, York, Leeds and Sheffield to Plymouth, Paignton and Bristol. To the railway enthusiast on holiday in the West Country they provide a welcome relief to the procession of Western Region class 50's and 47's along the photogenic sea wall stretch of line from Dawlish to Teignmouth.

The 'Peaks' are generally popular with enthusiasts and given the choice, many drivers favour them for their performance with heavily loaded trains, compared with other classes.

Throughout their years they have been worked hard and given excellent service and any future withdrawals will no doubt be met with great regret.

Keith Montague 1978

CLASS 44 PEAKS

Introduced:	1959 (Built at Derby)		Transmission:		Electric. Six Crompton Parkinson 305 hp axle-hung nose-suspended traction motors.
Engine:	Sulzer 12 cyl. 12 LDA 28A twin bank pressure charged of 2300 bhp at 750 rpm.				
Max Tractive Effort:	50,000 lb at 20% adhesion		Driving Wheel Diameter:		3' 9"
Weight:	133 tons.		Route Availability:		7
Fuel Capacity:	790 galls.		Maximum Speed:		90 mph
			Brake Force:		63 tons.

New Number	Original Number	Name	New Number	Original Number	Name
44 001	1	Scafell Pike	44 006	6	Whernside
44 002	2	Helvellyn	44 007	7	Ingleborough
44 003	3	Skiddaw	44 008	8	Penyghent
44 004	4	Great Gable	44 009	9	Snowdon
44 005	5	Cross Fell	44 010	10	Tryfan

Plate 1: The first of the Peaks No. D1 *Scafell Pike* posing for the camera at Derby, just after building in 1959.

British Rail

Construction

The following series of official photographs were taken at Derby and illustrate the building of a 'Peak' class locomotive from the first assembly to the finished product.

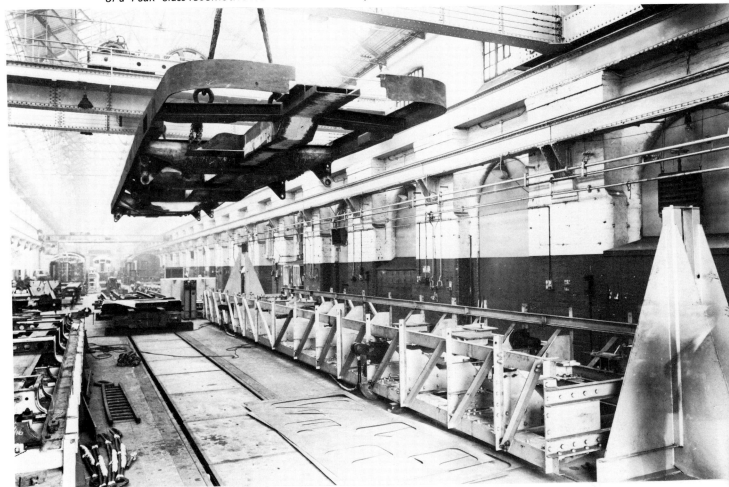

Plate 2: The underframe is lowered into place by one of the overhead gantry cranes.

Plate 3: The underframe complete with sideframes and bulkheads.

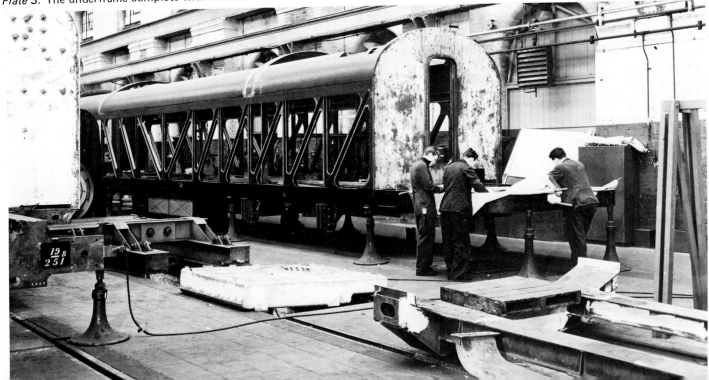

Plate 4: Interior assembly goes ahead.

Plate 5: An overhead gantry crane lowers the 'Sulzer 12 cylinder engine' and Crompton Parkinson transmission equipment.

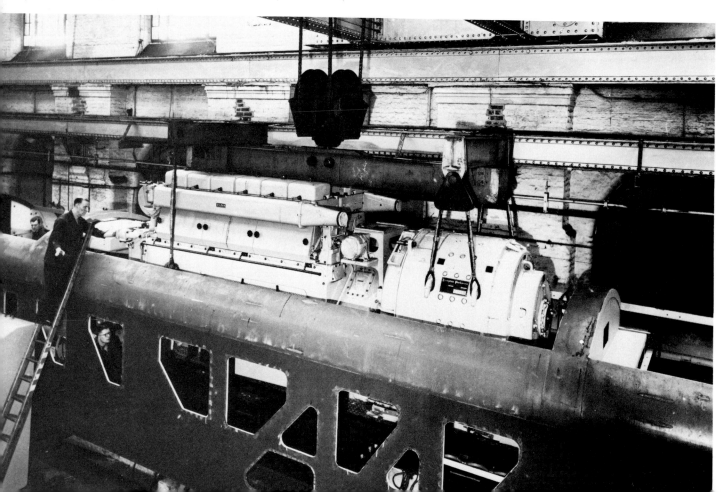

Plate 6: The bogies are positioned, to enable the main locomotive assembly to be lifted and fitted onto them.

Plate 7: Now on the 'middle road' No. D1 *Scafell Pike* takes on the look of a locomotive.

Plate 8: Nearing completion, but still with plenty of work to be done, the engineers start assembling the various cab fittings.

Plate 9: A very smart finished product, well worth all those painstaking hours of construction.

Early Liveries

Plate 10: The green livery first carried by the Peak Class 44 locomotives is clearly shown in this photograph of No. D1 *Scafell Pike* just after building.

British Rail

Plate 11: An up local service to Euston, consisting of suburban non-corridor stock passes near to Watford late in 1962, with class 44 No. D5 *Cross Fell* leading the way, presumably on a 'running-in' turn.

British Rail

Progression in Liveries

Plate 12: Toton Depot on 7th July 1971 with Peak class 44 locomotive No. 7 *Ingleborough* in green livery after losing the D from its number, and No. D2 *Helvellyn* behind.

N. Preedy

Plate 13: Class 44 Peak No. 4 *Great Gable* seen here in blue livery heading south on a freight working through Oxford on 15th August 1973.

G. Gamble

Renumbered locomotives at Toton
(Home of the 44's)

Plate 14: Nose to nose, two class 44's, Nos. 44 010 *Tryfan* and 44 006 *Whernside* stand in the shed yard at Toton, home of the 44's, on 7th June 1976.

G.W. Morrison

Plate 15: Line up of renumbered Peak class 44's at Toton on 11th July 1976 with Nos. 44 005, 44 002, 44 007 and 44 004, by this time bereft of nameplates.

G.W. Morrison

Class 44's on freight

Plate 16: No. 44 004 *Great Gable* minus her nameplates is seen here heading the evening Bescot to Tinsley freight north of Westhouses on 26th May 1977.

L.P. Gater

Plate 17: An interested spectator watches as No. 44 002 *Helvellyn* passes on an evening freight at Pye Bridge on 25th May 1977. The prominent space where she once carried her nameplate is very noticeable.

L.P. Gater

Plate 18: Toton based No. 44 004 *Great Gable* minus nameplates, working the 8V52 13.10 Toton to Westbury freight, is captured standing in Lansdown loop whilst No. 45 074 from the same depot passes with the 14.43 Leeds to Plymouth passenger service, on 26th August 1976.

B.J. Nicolle

Plate 19: Peak class No. 44 005 ex *Cross Fell*, (nameplates now gone), passes Crich Tramway Museum workshops at Clay Cross with an evening Bescot to Tinsley freight on 21st June 1977.

L.P. Gater

Plate 20: New number, nameplate and specifications of class 44 locomotive No. 44 003 *Skiddaw* are shown clearly here on this locomotive.

B. Morrison

Plate 21: Signal and Telegraph Department staff with their high-visibility jackets stand clear of the Down goods line as class 44 locomotive No. 44 003 *Skiddaw* passes near Burton on Trent with a mixed freight train on 18th September 1974.

A. Wynn

Plate 22: Close up view of No. 44 008 number and nameplate at Toton depot on 9th May 1976.

L.P. Gater

Plate 23: Class 44 locomotive No. 44 008 *Penyghent* in action on the outskirts of Burton on Trent with a coal train on 25th March 1975.

A. Wynn

In profile

Odd man out

Plate 24: Class 44 locomotive No. 44 009 *Snowdon* passes on freight near Burton on Trent on 24th June 1975. Note the indicator panel peculiar to this locomotive — the only one in the class fitted with this style. The remainder of the class were fitted with disc type headcodes as was the other end of this locomotive.

A. Wynn

Plate 25: This photograph of No. 44 009 *Snowdon* taken at Toton depot on 31st August 1975 shows the other end of the locomotive with the conventional class 44 disc type headcodes.

B. Morrison

44's on Enthusiasts' Specials

Plate 26: Enthusiasts' special 'The Peaks Express' headed by No. 44 008 *Penyghent* passes Torside crossing on this London to Manchester excursion on 1st October 1977.

I. Harrison

Plate 27: Double-headed Peak class 44 Nos. 44 005 *Cross Fell* and 44 002 *Helvellyn* pass near the famous crooked spire of Chesterfield on an enthusiasts' special on 24th July 1977.

I. Harrison

Plate 28: Class 44 locomotive No. 44 004 *Great Gable* takes the Derby/Birmingham main line at Stenson Junction with the outward L.C.G.B. (N.W.) 'Peak Commemorative Railtour' on a round trip from Liverpool. This train travelled to Manchester, Burton, Birmingham (Camp Hill loop), Leicester and Tinsley amongst many other places on 23rd April 1977, before returning to Liverpool.

L.P. Gater

CLASS 45 PEAKS

Introduced:	1960 (Built at Crewe & Derby)
Engine:	Sulzer 12 cyl. 12 LDA 28B twin bank with inter-cooling of 2500 bhp at 750 rpm.
Max Tractive Effort:	45/0 55,000 lb at 22.1% adhesion
	45/1 55,000 lb at 22.5% adhesion
Weight:	136 tons.
Fuel Capacity:	790 galls.

Transmission:	Electric. Six Crompton Parkinson 305 hp axle-hung nose suspended traction motors.
Driving Wheel Diameter:	3' 9"
Route Availability:	7
Maximum Speed:	90 mph
Brake Force:	63 tons.

Class 45/1 locomotives are fitted with electric train heating equipment only.

CLASS 45/0

New Number	Original Number	New Number	Original Number	New Number	Original Number	New Number	Original Number
45 001	13	45 021	25	*45 040	50	*45 059	98
45 002	29	*45 022	60	*45 041	53	*45 060	100
45 003	133	*45 023	54	45 042	57	45 061	101
*45 004	77	45 024	17	*45 043	58	45 062	103
45 005	79	45 025	19	*45 044	63	45 063	104
*45 006	89	45 026	21	*45 045	64	45 064	105
45 007	119	45 027	24	*45 046	68	45 065	110
45 008	90	45 028	27	45 047	69	45 066	114
45 009	37	45 029	30	*45 048	70	45 067	115
45 010	112	45 030	31	*45 049	71	45 068	118
45 011	12	45 031	36	45 050	72	45 069	121
45 012	108	45 032	38	45 051	74	45 070	122
45 013	20	45 033	39	45 052	75	45 071	125
*45 014	137	45 034	42	45 053	76	45 072	127
45 015	14	45 035	44	45 054	95	45 073	129
45 016	16	45 036	45	*45 055	84	45 074	131
45 017	23	45 037	46	45 056	91	45 075	132
45 018	15	45 038	48	45 057	93	45 076	134
45 019	33	*45 039	49	45 058	97	45 077	136
45 020	26						

CLASS 45/1

New Number	Original Number	New Number	Original Number
45 101	96	45 138	92
45 102	51	45 139	109
45 103	116	45 140	102
*45 104	59	45 141	82
45 105	86	45 142	83
45 106	106	*45 143	62
45 107	43	*45 144	55
45 108	120	45 145	128
45 109	85	45 146	66
45 110	73	45 147	41
*45 111	65	45 148	130
*45 112	61	45 149	135
45 113	80	45 150	78
45 114	94		(45 054)
45 115	81		
45 116	47		
45 117	35		
*45 118	67		
45 119	34		
45 120	107		
45 121	18		
45 122	11		
*45 123	52		
45 124	28		
45 125	123		
45 126	32		
45 127	87		
45 128	113		
45 129	111		
45 130	117		
45 131	124		
45 132	22		
45 133	40		
45 134	126		
*45 135	99		
45 136	88		
*45 137	56		

* Named Locomotives

Plate 30: Holbeck on 6th March 1961 with Peaks Nos. D35 and D93 behind on the stop-blocks. Steam locomotive No. 45569 'Jubilee' class 4-6-0 *Tasmania* shows its smokebox door to the right of the picture.

G.W. Morrison

Plate 31: Speeding through the cutting near Otterburn with the Down 'Thames-Clyde Express' complete with distinctive headboard is No. D15 on 29th June 1961.

G.W. Morrison

Plate 29: No. D100 *Sherwood Forester* appropriately carrying the head-board 'The Robin Hood' in green livery approaches St. Pancras Station from Nottingham on 26th September 1961. Note the old 17A Derby shed plate carried.

British Rail

Plate 32: Class 45 locomotive No. D39, heads a Bristol to Newcastle train under cautionary signals to take the coast route at Northallerton on 30th March 1962.

G.W. Morrison

Plate 33: Out in the countryside at Mangotsfield, No. D104 trundles the 14.55 Bristol to Dringhouses freight past a parcels train just disappearing into the distance on 15th May 1962.

British Rail

Plate 34: With beautiful countryside and hills all around, the secondman on class 45 locomotive No. D102 inhales the fresh air whilst working the Up 'Thames-Clyde Express' near Ais Gill on 1st September 1962.

G.W. Morrison

Plate 35: Slowly does it! as class 45 locomotive No. D16 slowly manoeuvres round Whitehall curve with the Down 'Waverley' express on 6th June 1962. The carriage destination board is visible on the maroon coach next to the engine.

G.W. Morrison

Plate 36: With a smattering of snow still laying on the ground in places, Peak No. D113 wends its way over the conglomeration of tracks, approaching Leeds City with a Down parcels train on 19th February 1963.

J.S. Whiteley

Plate 37: The driver takes a breath of fresh air as No. D15 emits a cloud of smoky exhaust whilst working the Down 'Waverley' at Leeds Holbeck Low Level on 1st May 1962.

G.W. Morrison

Plate 38: No. D100 *Sherwood Forester* leaves Leeds City on 19th May 1963 with the Up 'Harrogate Sunday Pullman'. This locomotive was deputising for a Deltic which had become derailed in the station.

J.S. Whiteley

Plate 39: The 16.25 St Pancras to Manchester service eases through Cricklewood with class 45 locomotive No. D64 in charge, in July 1962. This engine was later named *Coldstream Guardsman*.

British Rail

Plate 40: The 11.25 St Pancras to Leicester train stands at St Pancras ready to depart behind class 45 locomotive No. D57 on a murky December day in 1964.

British Rail

Plate 41: Locomotive No. D50 *The King's Shropshire Light Infantry* arrives at Westbury on 3rd May 1968 with a haul of house coal concentration wagons.

G.R. Hounsell

Plate 42: Gloucester Eastgate Station on 4th February 1967, with No. D66 waiting for the time to reach 11.16 before departing with a Bristol to Newcastle service. Eastgate station has now closed and trains go via the modernised Gloucester Central Station.

N. Preedy

Plate 43: Named Class 45 locomotive No. D84 *Royal Corps of Transport* stands at Gloucester Horton Road Depot on 16th July 1969.

N. Preedy

Plate 44: The Down 'Waverley' express passes the busy Wortley Junction on the outskirts of Leeds with No. D24 hauling this St Pancras — Edinburgh service on 20th September 1963. Steam is still in evidence in the form of a standard 2-6-0 3MT No. 77001 taking a rest between duties.

G.W. Morrison

Transition from Steam

Plate 45: The Down 'Thames-Clyde Express' passes Skipton North under clear signals, whilst 3F 0-6-0 tank engine No. 47577 stands waiting to let No. D11 and train speed on its way on 8th August 1962. No. D11 was the first of the unnamed 'Peaks' to enter service.

G.W. Morrison

Plate 46: Hatch open and in with 'the bag' to take water.

British Rail

Plate 47: Hang on, it's overflowing.

British Rail

Interesting and amusing photographs taken at Carlisle in the early 1960's with class 45 locomotive No. D99, since named *3rd Carabinier* being topped up with boiler water. The procedure of lifting a roof hatch to fill up from water columns has now been completely discontinued, with the roof hatches secured down and the foot holds on the side of the locomotive being sealed. The water intake is now done at buffer level.

45's in Blue Livery before renumbering

Plate 48: Study of the two types of class 45/0 headcode indicator panels at St Pancras station on 16th March 1974. To the left of the picture is No. D126 with the solid variety similar to that used on the class 46's and to the right is No. 122 with the split type of headcode panel.

B.J. Nicolle

Plate 49: Making its way towards Heron Close with a freight train from Toton to Westbury on 23rd January 1974 is class 45 locomotive No. D123.

B.J. Nicolle

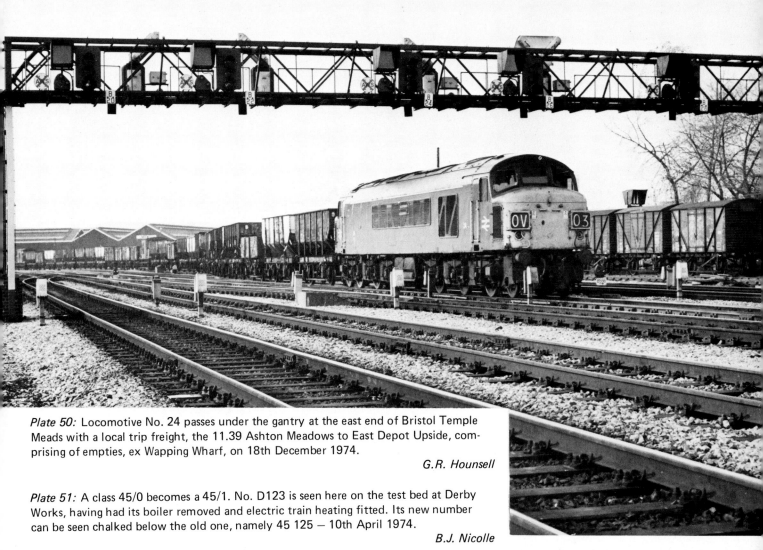

Plate 50: Locomotive No. 24 passes under the gantry at the east end of Bristol Temple Meads with a local trip freight, the 11.39 Ashton Meadows to East Depot Upside, comprising of empties, ex Wapping Wharf, on 18th December 1974.

G.R. Hounsell

Plate 51: A class 45/0 becomes a 45/1. No. D123 is seen here on the test bed at Derby Works, having had its boiler removed and electric train heating fitted. Its new number can be seen chalked below the old one, namely 45 125 — 10th April 1974.

B.J. Nicolle

Plate 52: A busy summer's afternoon in September 1974 at Cleethorpes. The signal is 'off'
for the adjoining line as class 45 locomotive No. 36 awaits departure with an excursion
to Nuneaton.

B.J. Nicolle

Plate 53: Leeds Holbeck based class 45 locomotive No. 30 powers away from Cheltenham
Spa station in brilliant sunshine on 26th October 1973, with the 13.21 Liverpool to
Plymouth train. The sun is so bright that the secondman has had to use newspaper as an
improvised sun-shade.

B.J. Nicolle

Plate 54: Holbeck depot, Leeds, showing class 45 locomotive No. D134 in green livery on 13th March 1961.

G. W. Morrison

Plate 55: Class 45 Peak locomotive No. 45 044 *Royal Inniskilling Fusilier* seen here standing outside Toton depot on 8th July 1976.

G. W. Morrison

Plate 56: Peaks at York — Class 46 diesel No. 46 046 and Class 45 No. D101 change over at York Station before taking a "Special" on to Scarborough on 18th May 1974.

G. W. Morrison

◄ *Plate 57:* A wet, cold, dark afternoon at Derby with locomotive No. 100 *Sherwood Forester* preparing to leave with a service to St Pancras on 4th February 1974.

B.J. Nicolle

◄ *Plate 58:* The distinctive architecture of Exeter St Davids makes a photogenic setting for this picture which was taken on 15th July 1972 and shows 1V85, the 10.45, Saturdays only, Manchester to Paignton train about to depart with locomotive No. 97 in charge.

N. Preedy

Plate 59: Locomotive No. 127 at the head of the 16.20 St Pancras to Sheffield train bursts forth from Elstree Tunnel on 16th June 1973.

B. Morrison

Plate 60: Peak Class 46 No. 46 050 passes beneath a fine display of semaphore signals with the up Kings Cross train at Black Carr Junction, Doncaster, on 30th January 1977.

G. W. Morrison

Plate 61: Approaching the junction at Shipley with the down Nottingham to Glasgow train, Peak No. 45 012 is seen here heading this express on 24th June 1976.

G. W. Morrison

Plate 62: Class 45 locomotive No. 98 *Royal Engineer* climbs the famous Lickey incline, located between Bromsgrove and Blackwell, with 1M72 the 10.30 Taunton to Manchester service on 27th October 1973.   *G.R. Hounsell*

Plate 63: Coal hopper wagons bound for the Southern Region passing Elstree headed by class 45 Peak No. 104.

                                                                                              B. Morrison

Plate 64: Class 45 locomotive No. D67 *The Royal Artilleryman* on the 08.50 Nottingham to St Pancras service is captured about to dive into Elstree Tunnel on 16th June 1973. The fast and slow lines go through separate tunnel bores and the slow lines can be seen on the right of the picture, with Elstree station visible to the rear of the train.

B. Morrison

Plate 65: The 10.30 Paignton to Leeds and Hull train leaves Burton on Trent headed by Class 45 No. 76 on 29th June 1974.

A. Wynn

Class 45 Naming

Certain locomotives in this class have been named and many of these names were originally carried by locomotives of the 'Royal Scot' and 'Patriot' classes of the London Midland & Scottish Railway.

Named locomotives in the Peak class 45 are listed below:

New Number	Original Number	Name	New Number	Original Number	Name
45 039	49	The Manchester Regiment	45 045	64	Coldstream Guardsman
45 040	50	King's Shropshire Light Infantry	45 111	65	Grenadier Guardsman
45 123	52	The Lancashire Fusilier	45 118	67	The Royal Artilleryman
45 041	53	Royal Tank Regiment	45 046	68	Royal Fusilier
45 023	54	The Royal Pioneer Corps	45 048	70	The Royal Marines
45 144	55	Royal Signals	45 049	71	The Staffordshire Regiment (The Prince of Wales's)
45 137	56	The Bedfordshire and Hertfordshire Regiment (T.A.)	45 004	77	Royal Irish Fusilier
45 043	58	The King's Own Royal Border Regiment	45 055	84	Royal Corps of Transport
45 104	59	The Royal Warwickshire Fusilier	45 006	89	Honourable Artillery Company
45 022	60	Lytham St. Annes	45 059	98	Royal Engineer
45 112	61	Royal Army Ordnance Corps	45 135	99	3rd Carabinier
45 143	62	5th Royal Inniskilling Dragoon Guards	45 060	100	Sherwood Forester
45 044	63	Royal Inniskilling Fusilier	45 014	137	The Cheshire Regiment

Plate 66: An unusual visitor to Broad Street station on a unique occasion with pomp and ceremony. No. D89 arrives on 9th June 1965 with newly installed nameplate about to be unveiled, marking the naming of the locomotive *Honourable Artillery Company*.

British Rail

Class 45 Nameplates

Plates 67, 68, 69, 70, 71, 72: Photographs by N. Preedy, G.R. Hounsell, and C.L. Caddy.

THE CHESHIRE REGIMENT

SHERWOOD FORESTER

GRENADIER GUARDSMAN

Named 45's at work

Plate 73: No. 45 048 *The Royal Marines* passes Hasland heading the 14.43 Leeds-Plymouth Express on 23rd July 1976.

L.P. Gater

Plate 74: A famous photographic location is Parsons Tunnel between Dawlish and Teignmouth. Here the 09.02 Leicester to Paignton train headed by Peak No. 45 039 *The Manchester Regiment* emerges into the daylight on 2nd August 1975.

N. Preedy

Plate 75: No. 45 043 *The King's Own Royal Border Regiment* is seen here marshalling stock at Laira, Plymouth on 15th August 1976.

L.P. Gater

Plate 76: A returning excursion from Scarborough rounds the curve at Kirkham Abbey on 4th July 1976, with No. 45 004 *Royal Irish Fusilier* leading the way.

G.W. Morrison

Plate 77: Peak No. 45 039 *The Manchester Regiment* hammers along at a great rate of knots with the seven coach 17.38 Leeds to Bristol service on 5th July 1976, seen here emerging from Ardsley Tunnel.

G.W. Morrison

Plate 78: A somewhat desolate setting, with No. 45 040 *King's Shropshire Light Infantry* heading the 09.05 Leeds to Glasgow train across Dandry Mire Viaduct, north of Garsdale on 13th September 1976.

T.G. Flinders

Plate 79: Toton motive power depot showing class 44 No. 44 010 *Tryfan* devoid of nameplates on 8th July 1976.

G. W. Morrison

Plate 80a: Nameplate of locomotive No. 45 049 *The Staffordshire Regiment (The Prince of Wales's)* clearly showing the regimental crest.

A. D. Coombe

Plate 80: Class 45 locomotive No. 45 049 *The Staffordshire Regiment (The Prince of Wales's)* stands at Exeter St. David's Station awaiting departure for Paignton on 9th September 1976.

A. D. Coombe

Plate 81: Class 45 locomotive No. 45 033 passes through Cowley Bridge Junction with a down freight headed for Exeter Riverside on 8th September 1976.

A. D. Coombe

Plate 82: The recently constructed bridge between Winterbourne and Bristol Parkway over the M4 Motorway provides the setting for this photograph of locomotive No. 45 023 *The Royal Pioneer Corps* with a Down passenger working on 26th February 1977.

G.R. Hounsell

Plate 83: Class 45 locomotive No. 45 048 *The Royal Marines* passes Alston sidings near Cheltenham with 6V15 which on 13th May 1976, was the 14.46 Great Bridge to Llandeilo Junction steel train.

B.J. Nicolle

Freight Workings

Plate 84: A heavily loaded coal train comes down the incline from the North London line and into the Yard at Acton on 12th October 1976, with class 45 locomotive No. 45 056 wending its way.

M. Woodward

Plate 85: Captured at Burton on Trent with the aid of a tele-photo lens, locomotive No. 45 067 heads a coal train on the down main line through the station on 13 April 1977.

A. Wynn

Plate 86: A scene at Kings Cross station showing class 46 locomotive No. 46 014 departing with the 10.45 express to Newcastle on 10th July 1976. The stabling point can be seen on the right.

G. W. Morrison

Plate 88: Passing through Blackburn Meadows, near Rotherham, Class 45 No. 45 013 heads the 10.12 Newcastle to Cardiff train on 2nd June 1977.

G. W. Morrison

Plate 87: A wet night at Plymouth — Peak No. 45 065 passes through Plymouth North Road Station with the 18.05 St. Blazey-Stoke on Trent night freight on 2nd November 1976.

A. D. Coombe

Plate 89: Complete with sealed beam marker lights in place of reporting numbers, class 45 engine No. 45 071 passes Holbeck Junction, Leeds with a train of ballast, with gypsies camping on the waste ground to the right of the picture.

G.W. Morrison

Plate 90: Peak class locomotive No. 45 021 passes Barrow Hill with an Up freight on 22nd November 1977.

L.P. Gater

Awaiting departure

Plate 91: Locomotive No. 45 130 prepares to depart from Nottingham Midland station on 28th June 1974 with the 12.50 service to St Pancras.

B.J. Nicolle

Plate 93: Topping up with coolant at Bristol Temple Meads on 10th November 1976, class 45 locomotive No. 45 005 is almost ready to depart with a train bound for Newcastle.

G. Scott-Lowe

Plate 94: The 11.05 St Pancras to Sheffield train consisting of air-conditioned coaching stock pauses at Nottingham Midland station on 12th August 1975, with locomotive No. 45 132 on duty.

N. Preedy

◄ *Plate 92:* The driver of No. 45 110 looks back along the 10.50 Nottingham to St Pancras train at Leicester platform number 3a on 4th June 1976 to await the 'right away' from the guard.

B.J. Nicolle

45's in Yorkshire

Plate 95: Two class 45's leave simultaneously from Leeds City Station carrying two different styles of route indicator panels. One leaves for Liverpool, the other for Kings Cross.

E. Sanderson

Plate 96: Rather an interesting photograph showing class 45 No. 45 009 gingerly rounding the curve at Shipley Bingley Junction on a Nottingham to Glasgow train on 30th July 1976.

G.W. Morrison

Plate 97: Class 45 locomotive No. 45 025 rounds the bend at Clifton on the outskirts of York with the 11.30 Edinburgh to Plymouth cross-country service on 26th September 1976.

J.S. Whiteley

Plate 98: With the beautiful city of York in the background, class 45 locomotive No. 45 024 approaches Holgate Junction having just brought the 14.42 (Sundays) Newcastle to Poole train from under the overall York station roof on 26th September 1976.

J.S. Whiteley

Plate 101: The scene at Sheffield ▶ Midland station on Sunday, 7th April 1974 with class 45 locomotive No. 45 113 preparing to leave with 1M21, a Leeds to St Pancras service, diverted due to engineering works north of Chesterfield.

B.J. Nicolle

Plate 102: The 15.58 Newcastle to ▶ Liverpool train coasts down the bank past Batley, behind class 45 locomotive No. 45 012 on 25th June 1976 with a local service diesel multiple unit just about to come into the picture climbing in the opposite direction.

G.W. Morrison

Plate 99: Peak class locomotive No. 45 047 pulls away light from Leeds City Station.

E. Sanderson

Plate 100: An engineers' ballast train, headed by class 45 locomotive No. 45 073 rounds the curve passing through Rodley Cutting near Leeds on 21st July 1975.

G.W. Morrison

... and in Derbyshire

Around London...

Plate 105: A coal train bound for the Southern Region approaches Elstree Tunnel with class 45 locomotive No. 119 at the head, on 16th June 1973.

B. Morrison

◀ *Plate 103:* Class 45 locomotive passes through the sunlit Pennines in Edale, Derbyshire heading the Manchester to Harwich boat train on Saturday, 12th March 1977.

I. Harrison

◀ *Plate 104:* Return excursion train to St. Pancras hauled by locomotive No. 45 070 with empty stock arrives at Matlock (pay train branch) on 24th August 1975.

L.P Gater

46´s on freight

Plate 149: Gateshead based class 46 locomotive No. 191 powers 6Z31 return empty cement Pres-flows special from Uddingston to Northfleet, through Grantham station on 12th September 1973.

B.J. Nicolle

Plate 150: Locomotive class 46 No. 165 approaches Westbury with a train of stone empties for Merehead Quarry on 22nd June 1973, whilst a loaded train disappears into the distance on the adjoining track.

G.R. Hounsell

Plate 147: In ex-works condition, class 46 locomotive No. 46 015 makes its way towards Badgeworth Road Bridge near Churchdown with a special coal train from Toton to South Wales on 29th May 1974.

B.J. Nicolle

Plate 148: Class 46 No. 46 008 approaches Westbury off the Trowbridge line with a mineral train on 23rd August 1977. The removal of the indicator panel has left this locomotive with a very plain front end.

D.H. Allen

Plate 151: Locomotive No. 46 029 trundles through Peterborough station on 1st June 1976 with the 12.25 Northfleet to Uddingston, Block Blue Circle cement train.

B.J. Nicolle

Plate 152: An Up mixed freight train headed by locomotive No. 46 008 passes Swindon Locomotive, Carriage and Wagon Works on 24th June 1976.

B. Morrison

Plate 153: Locomotive No. 46 054 prepares to leave Kingsland Road Full Loads Depot on 5th August 1975 with a midday local freight train bound for Swindon and calling only at Chippenham for traffic purposes.

B.J. Nicolle

Plate 154: Peak No. 46 024 is seen here trundling towards Gloucester with the 04.27 Stoke on Trent to St Blazey 'Clayliner' train on 13th February 1974.

B.J. Nicolle

46's in the West Country...

Plate 156: Heading along the sea wall near Teignmouth class 46 locomotive No. 46 032 ▶ powers a summer Saturdays only working, the 10.05 Newquay to Newcastle train, on 22nd June 1974.

N. Preedy

Plate 157: Peak No. 46 042 passes Taunton at speed on an express from the north on ▶ 15th May 1976.

C.L. Caddy

Plate 158: No. 46 003 arrives at Bristol Temple Meads (platform 7) with 1M88, the 06.25
Plymouth to Liverpool service, whilst No. 31 256 occupies platform 4 with empty
coaching stock bound for Malago Vale carriage sidings on 25th March, 1975.

G.R. Hounsell

Plate 159: Locomotive No. 46 022 rescues No. 47 090 *Vulcan* after failing with the 14.00
Penzance to Birmingham train on 6th March 1976. The train is seen here entering St
Austell station.

N. Preedy

Plate 160: At Dawlish Warren we capture the 15.35, Saturdays only, Paignton to Birmingham service on 22nd June 1976 powered by class 46 locomotive No. 46 050.

N. Preedy

Plate 161: Class 46 locomotive No. 46 028 in charge of the 11.35 (Sundays) Penzance to Leeds train on 1st September 1974, passing through Liskeard station, deep in the heart of Cornwall.

N. Preedy

...and in Wales

Plate 162: Peak No. 46 015, with a party of enthusiasts from the Bath Branch of the Locomotive Club of Gt. Britain in the brake vans, calls at Waun-Lwyd (between Duffryn Yard and Cwm) for wagons to be attached for the return journey to Severn Tunnel Junction on 10th May 1975.

G.R. Hounsell

Plate 163: Locomotive No. 46 024 heads a train of empty coal hoppers over the River Usk into Newport.

British Rail

Plate 164: Peak No. D159 descends from Bishton Flyover (in the background) to the level of the Newport – Severn Tunnel main line at Llandevenny with a class 46 'fitted' freight train on 2nd October 1971.

G.R. Hounsell

Plate 165: Industrial South Wales – No. 46 015 berths the 08.20 Severn Tunnel Junction to Ebbw Vale freight on arrival at its destination on 10th May 1975.

G.R. Hounsell

46's around Yorkshire

Plate 168: Peak No. 46 006 enters Rotherham on 30th May 1974 with the Bristol to Edinburgh express.

A.J. Booth

Plate 169: The 10.02 Newcastle to Liverpool train emerges into the sunlight from the tunnel at Springwood Junction, Huddersfield on 25th August 1975 with No. 46 053 providing the motive power.

G.W. Morrison

Plate 166: Gateshead allocated class 46 No. 46 031 arrives at platform 14, York with the 07.30 Birmingham (New St.) to Newcastle on 30th April 1977.

L.P. Gater

Plate 167: Gateshead based class 46 number 46 038 accelerates away from Doncaster past the NCL depot, with a Leeds to Kings Cross passenger train in March 1975.

B.J. Nicolle

Plate 172: With the 'banner off' for a train in the opposite direction, No. 46 031 passes ▶
Heaton Lodge near Mirfield with the 18.10 Liverpool to Newcastle train on 21st August
1976.

G.W. Morrison

Plate 170: The 17.10 Liverpool to Newcastle train headed by No. 46 050, crosses Batley
Viaduct in the evening sun on 30th June 1975.

G.W. Morrison

Plate 171: The 10.02 Newcastle to Liverpool service passes the vandalised and desolate
steam depot at Mirfield on 3rd July 1975, headed by class 46 locomotive No. 46 030.

G.W. Morrison

Plate 173: Locomotive No. 46 044 passes the buttress of the old Midland line viaduct approaching Bradley Junction near Huddersfield on the 10.10 Liverpool to Newcastle express on 8th August 1976.

G.W. Morrison

Nationwide Passenger Workings

Plate 174: Peak No D169 makes ready to depart from Leeds Central with the Up 'Yorkshire Pullman' on 15th April 1967. These comfortable Pullman cars are amongst the few still used today.

G.W. Morrison

Plate 175: Locomotive No. 46 055 puts up a good exhaust whilst accelerating near Linthwaite with the 10.02 Newcastle to Liverpool train on 31st July 1976. Class 25 locomotive No. 25 114 passes on a summer Saturdays only Llandudno to Leeds working.

G.W. Morrison

Plate 176: King's Cross station on 10th July 1976 with Cardiff based locomotive No. 46 014 departing on a Newcastle bound train. The suburban
station can be seen to the right of the picture, with the St Pancras
Chambers tower marking the far side of St Pancras station. The Deltic locomotive just visible in the photograph is on the fuelling depot. A new and
simplified approach layout has now been introduced at King's Cross
reducing the 'bottleneck' effect which had hitherto tended to cause delays.
G.W. Morrison

Plate 177: The Down 'Devonian' 10.40 Leeds to Paignton is about to pass
over Brockhampton Level Crossing, near Swindon village on 29th May
1974, headed by No. 46 024. *B.J. Nicolle*

Plate 178: The 17.10 Liverpool to Newcastle train approaches Thornhill Junction near Dewsbury, behind class 46 locomotive No. 46 053 on 21st August 1976.

G.W. Morrison

Plate 179: A Newcastle to Liverpool working climbing out of Huddersfield, through Paddock with its steep sheer rock face towering above, on 14th June 1974 with locomotive No. 46 047 providing the traction.

G.W. Morrison

Plate 180: The 09.53 Sheffield–Paignton train leaves Whiteball Tunnel under a clear semaphore signal and passes the little signal box controlling this stretch of line on 29th May 1976. Motive power is provided by class 46 locomotive No. 46 047.

G. Scott-Lowe

Plate 181: Class 46 locomotive No. 46 022 is captured in Winterbourne cutting with the 09.15 Birmingham to Taunton service on 27th April 1975.

G.R. Hounsell

Plate 182: Locomotive No. 46 048 here in charge of the 09.25 Birmingham to Paignton train on 29th May 1976, pictured climbing towards Whiteball Tunnel.

G. Scott-Low

Plate 183: A somewhat unusual picture with locomotive No. 46 055 on the 10.02 Newcastle to Liverpool train, being pushed up the bank by a following train near Marsden after failing completely. The cavalcade consists of No. 46 055 and ten coaches pushed by locomotive No. 40 154 with another nine coaches, on 31st July 1976.

G.W. Morrison

Plate 184: The scene just outside Chesterfield on 22nd September 1974, with No. 46 022 leading the 12.51, Sundays only, Newcastle to Plymouth train.

N. Preedy

Plate 185: Peak No. 46 035 leaves Bristol Parkway Station with the 09.00 Paignton to Newcastle express on Saturday, 17th August 1974.

N. Preedy

Plate 188: Amidst attractive countryside on a sunny October day in 1976, class 46 locomotive No. 46 048 hauls the 09.55 Edinburgh to Plymouth train near Croft.

J.S. Whiteley

Plate 186: A plume of smoke rises as No. 46 013 leaves Bristol Temple Meads with a
Leeds to Paignton cross country train on 4th July 1976.

G. Scott-Lowe

Plate 187: Gloucester Horton Road Crossing with the 14.23 Manchester to Cardiff express
headed by No. 46 007 approaching Gloucester station on 14th May 1974.

N. Preedy

Plate 189: Class 46 037 heads down the Exe estuary and prepares to pass through
Dawlish Warren with the 08.20 Birmingham to Plymouth train on 19th August 1977.

D.H. Allen

Peaks in the night...

Plate 190: A dark wet evening in January 1962 at St Pancras with the 17.25 St Pancras to Nottingham train 'The Robin Hood' standing at platform 6. Just before departure the guard 'takes the tally' and has a word with the driver of locomotive No. D124, diagrammed to haul the train.

British Rail

Plate 191: Bristol Temple Meads on 9th October 1976. The 13.25 from Edinburgh and 13.35 from Glasgow Central which combines at Carstairs, arrives at its final destination with locomotive No. 45 021 up front.

G. Scott-Lowe

Plate 192: Another night scene, this time under the overhead wires at Birmingham New Street. Class 45 No. 45 016 waits to depart with the 14.35 Paignton to York service on 21st December 1974, whilst a class 87 electric locomotive stands in one of the adjoining platforms. Note that the headcode on the York train should be 1E70 and not 4E32. *N. Preedy*

Plate 193: On a dark winter's evening in November 1975 a return special excursion waits at York station for the journey back to London. The locomotive, complete with illuminated headcode, allocated for the duty is class 46 No. 46 043 and immaculate it looks against the background of the fluorescent station lights. *N. Preedy*

...and in Landscape

Plate 194: The up 'Cornishman' crossing the River Derwent at Broadholme, south of Ambergate, headed by an unidentified Peak on 26th June 1976.

L.P. Gater

Plate 195: The picturesque setting for this attractive photograph is Morley Low near Leeds. The 07.55 Newcastle to Liverpool train passes through the short platform and into Morley Tunnel on 1st July 1976. *G.W. Morrison*

Plate 196: An unidentified class 45 locomotive heads an up afternoon express at Ambergate Junction on 23rd May 1975. *L.P. Gater*

Peaks on works...

Plate 197: The Locomotive Works Erecting Shop on 18th January 1975, with No. 45 149 nearing completion stage, to return once more to the main line.

N. Preedy

Plate 198: The body of Peak class 46 locomotive No. 182 hovers above its frame in the erecting shop at Derby Locomotive Works during the Open Day on Saturday 29th August 1970.

G.R. Hounsell

Plate 199: Peak No. 46 026 together with other members of the same class undergoes heavy maintenance at Derby Works on 16th November 1975.

G. Scott-Lowe

Plate 200: Toton allocated class 45 No. 45 077 drys out after a repaint at Derby Works on 7th May 1977.

L.P. Gater

...and on Shed

MIDLAND REGION

EASTERN REGION

◄ Plate 201: Named class 45 No. 45 044 *Royal Inniskilling Fusilier* amongst class 47's and No. 44 002 *Helvellyn* at Toton motive power depot on 8th July 1976.

G.W. Morrison

◄ Plate 202: Class 45 No. 45 022 *Lytham St. Annes* leaves York motive power depot to head a Scotland bound express on 21st September 1975. Note the glimpse of the past in the background with a museum destined Great Western locomotive awaiting transfer.

B. Morrison

Plate 203: Class 46 locomotive No. 46 043 stands off duty on a Sunday at Haymarket Depot, Edinburgh.

D.R. Kennedy

SCOTTISH REGION

Plate 204: Peak No. 45 075 stands at Laira Depot amongst a variety of locomotives on 22nd February 1976.

D.M. Habgood

WESTERN REGION

Inside information

Driving cab layout

As is standard on BR diesels the driver sits at the left with a seat for the driver's assistant on the right. The driver's controls are located on a desk; on the left are the locomotive brake and train brake controls and to the right a large lever fitted with a hand grip which is the power handle. This incorporates a button which operates the anti-slip brake by making a small application of the locomotive air brake. Immediately to the left of the power handle is the master handle which has four positions: *Off, Forward, engine only* and *reverse*. When moved to *engine only* power cannot be applied to the traction motors.

On the instrument panel in front of the driver are:

Vacuum brake pipe/reservoir gauge
Brake cylinder pressure gauge
Main reservoir pressure gauge
Brake pipe pressure gauge (not Class 44s)
Driving ammeter (this indicates the electric current strength being provided to the traction motors)
Fault indicator (blue light normally dim but becomes bright in the event of a fault)
Engine stopped indicator (normally a dim red light)
Wheel slip indicator (normally a dim amber light)
Speedometer

Beneath the driving desk is the pedal-operated driver's safety device.

To the left of the driver's assistant's seat is the hand brake wheel and on a panel in front of the seat either a steam pressure gauge and boiler fault indicator or electric train heating supply indicator dependent on whether the locomotive is fitted with steam or electric coach warming apparatus.

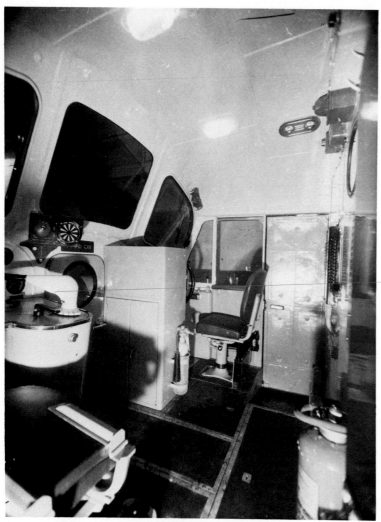

Plate 205: The interior of the driver's cab of No. D1 *Scafell Pike*, with the driver's position nearest the camera and secondman's seat to the right. The nose end communicating door can clearly be seen in the centre of the picture.

British Rail

Plate 206: The driver's position.

British Rail

Essential differences

The **Class 44** originally numbered D1-D10, now Nos. 44 001-44 010, was delivered in 1959-60 and the locomotives are of 2,300 bhp and of 1 Co-Co 1 wheel configuration. Powered by the Sulzer 12LDA28-A engine built in Switzerland at the Winterthur works of Sulzer, the Class 44 units have a starting tractive effort of 70,000 lb and a continuous tractive effort of 41,000 lb at 16.5 mph. Electrical equipment is by Crompton Parkinson the main generator providing power to six axle-hung traction motors each of 305 hp.

Although designed for both passenger and freight work, following introduction of the Class 45 in some numbers, the train heating boiler and water tanks in the Class 44 locomotives were removed and the ten locomotives were thereafter confined to freight work; this took place in 1962-3. The locomotives are all named after mountains in England and Wales from which followed the name 'Peak', also applied by analogy to the Class 45 and 46 locomotives. They are all based at Toton in Nottinghamshire. The Class 44s retain their gangway doors built in the nose at each end of the locomotive and intended for multiple operation.

The **Class 45** consists of 127 locomotives using the Sulzer 12LDA28-13 engine of 2,500 bhp and Crompton Parkinson electrical equipment giving a maximum tractive effort of 55,000 lb and a continuous tractive effort of 30,000 lb at 25 mph. Originally numbered D11-D127 they were renumbered 45 001-45 077 (steam heated) and 45 101-45 150 (electrically heated). The six axle-hung traction motors are each of 337 hp and the diesel engines were built by Vickers-Armstrong Ltd at Barrow under licence from Sulzer as were those of Class 46.

The **Class 46** consists of 56 locomotives and is basically similar to the Class 45 except that electrical equipment is by Brush instead of Crompton Parkinson. The 12LDA28-B diesel engine is fitted with a Brush TG 160-60 main generator which feeds six Brush TM 73-68 Mk III traction motors of 327 hp each.

Plate 207: The engine compartment of the locomotive in sparkling clean condition, just after building in 1959.

British Rail

GENERAL DATA	Class 44	Class 45	Class 46
Diesel engine	12LDA28-A (Sulzer)	12LDA28-B (Sulzer)	12LDA28-B (Sulzer)
Electrical equipment	Crompton Parkinson	Crompton Parkinson	Brush
Wheel arrangement	1 Co-Co 1	1 Co-Co 1	1 Co-Co 1
Maximum tractive effort	70,000 lb	55,000 lb	55,000 lb
Engine hp	2,300 hp @ 750 rpm	2,500 hp @ 750 rpm	2,500 hp @ 750 rpm
Length over buffers	67ft 11in	67ft 11in	67ft 11in
Width	9ft 1$\frac{9}{16}$ in	9ft 1$\frac{9}{16}$ in	9ft 1$\frac{9}{16}$ in
Height (rail to roof)	12ft 10½in	12ft 10½in	12ft 10½in
Total wheelbase	59ft 8in	59ft 8in	59ft 8in
Minimum radius curve	5 chains	5 chains	5 chains
Fuel capacity	840 gal.	840 gal	840 gal.
Boiler water capacity	—	1,040 gal.	1,040 gal.
Weight	138 tons 2 cwt	136 tons	137 tons 11 cwt
Top speed	90 mph	90 mph	90 mph
Built	Derby	Derby/Crewe	Derby/Crewe
Brake	Straight air (locomotive) Vacuum (train)	Straight air (locomotive) Dual air/vacuum (train)	Straight air (locomotive) Dual air/vacuum (train)

Above information based on British Rail data

As already mentioned the steam heating boilers in the Class 44s were removed some years ago. The Class 45/0 (45 001-45 077) are steam heated whilst the 45/1 locomotives (45 101-45 150) contain electric train heating equipment. The Class 46s only contain steam heating boilers.

British Rail Official Diagrams of the Peak Class

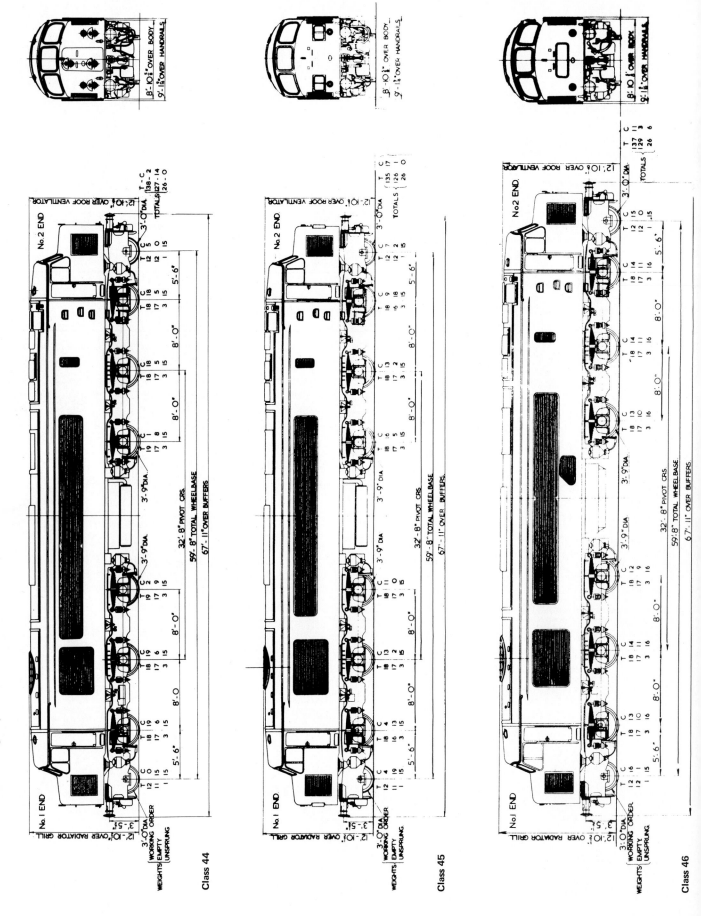

Class 44

Class 45

Class 46